THE MYSTERY OF
THE HIDDEN ARCHER

THE MYSTERY OF
THE HIDDEN ARCHER

STEVE SWANSON

ZondervanPublishingHouse
Grand Rapids, Michigan

A Division of HarperCollins*Publishers*

The Mystery of the Hidden Archer
Copyright 1994 by Steve Swanson

Requests for information should be addressed to:
Zondervan Publishing House
Grand Rapids, Michigan 49530

Library of Congress Cataloging-in-Publication Data

Swanson, Steve, 1932–
    The mystery of the hidden archer / Steve Swanson.
        p.cm.—(A Penny and Chad earthkeeper mystery; bk. 4)
    Summary: A tree planting trip to northern Minnesota presents an
opportunity to solve a mystery, right an old wrong, and save a life.
    ISBN 0-310-39831-2 (softcover)
    [1. Minnesota—Fiction. 2. Mystery and detective stories.]   I. Title.
II. Series : Swanson, Steve, 1932–   Earthkeepers series: bk. 4.
PZ7.S9725Myo   1994
[Fic]—dc20
                                    94-30702
                                            CIP
                                            AC

Edited by Dave Lambert
Cover design by Chris Gannon
Cover illustration by Doug Knutson
Interior design by Sue Koppenol
Interior illustrations by Tim Davis

Printed in the United States of America

94 95 96 97 98 99 00 01 02 /❖DH/ 10 9 8 7 6 5 4 3 2 1

 Printed on Recylced Paper

*My sincere thanks to
Ruth Geisler, Ron Klug, and Dave Lambert
for early encouragement and help,
and to Shelley Sateren for her many
critiques and suggestions.*

Contents

The Cedar Arrow

"Look at this," Mom said as the microwave buzzer went off, telling me my second bowl of Malt-O-Meal was ready.

"What?" I asked, opening the microwave door to take out the bowl.

"This story in the morning paper." She pushed the paper across the table to me. I read the headline: "MYSTERIOUS ARROW SAVES ABDUCTED WOMAN."

Good. I liked mysteries. Not as much as my friend Penny liked them, though. She was a maniac for mysteries. I started reading the story, and noticed a familiar town name.

"That town is up near Uncle Andrew's cabin, isn't it, Mom?"

"Yes, it is, right up by Bigfork. But that wasn't why I wanted you to read it. Look at the name of the woman."

As I was scanning the story for the name of the victim, Penny burst in the back door. Even a best friend like Penny usually knocks at least a little before she walks into our kitchen, but that morning she just burst in waving a newspaper.

"Did you see this?" she shouted, waving the paper at us.

"We were just looking," my mom said, giving Penny her usual loving pat on the cheek. "Tell Chad who the woman is."

"It's my Aunt Jean, that's who it is!" Penny exclaimed, almost jumping in her excitement.

"She had a narrow escape," Mom said.

"She sure did," Penny said. "Mom left for Grand Rapids last night. She's going to bring Aunt Jean home."

I still hadn't read the story yet. "So what happened?" I asked.

"Some mysterious forest person shot a kidnapper and saved my aunt," Penny said.

"He used a homemade cedar arrow," Mom added.

I had met Penny's Aunt Jean a year ago. Penny called her "my favorite aunt."

"An Indian?" I asked.

"Nobody knows," Penny said. "They found bear tracks all over the place."

"Wait—you mean a *bear* shot the arrow?"

"Just look," Penny said, pointing to the article on the table.

I scanned the article while Mom and Penny talked quietly.

MYSTERIOUS ARROW SAVES ABDUCTED WOMAN

A woman abducted Tuesday from a Minneapolis parking lot was found yesterday safe and unharmed in the Itasca National Forest. She escaped from her abductor near Bigfork in northern Minnesota. "He was about to hit me," Jean Palmer, 28, sobbed to Duluth reporters later in the day. "Then he just let go of me and grabbed his own leg." The Itasca County sheriff's office reported that the kidnapper had been shot in the leg by an unknown archer who used a homemade cedar arrow. Miss Palmer ran back along the logging road, then flagged down a highway maintenance truck on Minnesota 38. Sheriff's deputies later found the wounded kidnapper sitting in his car. Two tires had been shot flat, also with cedar arrows. The kidnapper was arrested and taken to Itasca County Hospital. Authorities puzzled over bear tracks that seemed to cover the scene. Deputy Don Carver reported, "Looks as if a bear followed that woman right out of the woods. He watched while she caught her ride on the highway, then that crazy bear turned right around and came back to the car. If I didn't know better" Carver said, "I'd say the bear shot out the tires." Area residents recalled an incident a year ago when a rabid dog that was threatening a young camper was shot through the neck with an identical arrow. Forest rangers had no comment but said they would assist in the investigation.

"Chad and I were just saying that his Uncle Andrew's cabin is up there near Bigfork," Mom said. "I'm going to get the map."

As the three of us were running our fingers over the northern half of a map of Minnesota, trying to figure out how close my uncle's cabin was to the crime scene, Penny said, "I think that's where our church Earthkeepers group is going to plant trees next month—in the Itasca National Forest."

"It's a big forest," Mom said. "Look." She traced a large green area with her finger. "It covers half of northern Minnesota."

"They're going to Marcell," Penny said, pointing to a town just south of Bigfork.

"They?" Mom asked. "You mean you aren't going?"

"I've been trying to talk Chad into going. If *he'll* go, I will."

"Oh, Chad—you *should* go," Mom said. "Did you know that's right up by Uncle Andrew's cabin?" Mom showed Penny, putting her fingernail just under a red spot on the shore of Horseshoe Lake. "I put that spot on two years ago when Chad and I planned to get up there—but never quite made it." Mom looked at me with that "I'm sorry" look on her face.

"Is he up there a lot, your Uncle Andrew?" Penny asked.

"Mostly in June," Mom said. "He says that's the best fishing month."

"Maybe we could see him if we went up tree planting," Penny suggested.

"Of *course* you could," Mom said smiling. "What a great idea. Maybe I could come up, too, and the three of us could stay a few extra days."

"That would be *great,*" Penny gushed. Anything she and my mom could do together was great with her. "Wouldn't it, Chad?"

"Yeah," I said, not sounding too excited. Mom noticed.

"What's wrong, Chad?" she asked.

12

"Oh, nothing," I said, not wanting to hurt her feelings. I didn't want to remember how many of our plans, Mom's and mine, had to be set aside because of Mom's real-estate business. We'd plan something fun, and get all excited about it, and then a real-estate deal would fall through—or maybe a new one would come up. Suddenly she'd get very busy. We just kept putting things off.

"So what's your Uncle Andrew like?" Penny asked as we rode briskly, side by side, toward school.

"Mom will never get up there, anyway. She'll be too busy."

"Don't be so grumpy. Anyway, what's that got to do with what he's like? What's he like, anyway?"

"He's a big guy. Chubby. Used to work for a bank. Hated it. Always wanted to move to the north woods."

"How is he your uncle? Is he your mom's brother?"

"My dad's brother. Sometimes all he and Mom can talk about is Dad."

"Is that so bad?"

"Makes my mom sad, that's all."

"Do you like him?"

"My dad?"

"No, your uncle."

"I do. I like him a lot. Sometimes I think that when we're together, he tries to make it up to me for what happened between Mom and Dad."

"That's nice of him."

"I guess. But I'd rather have my real dad back."

We parked our bikes and walked into the school. All I could think of were math tests and English tests— and after that, "Good-bye-for-the-summer" homeroom

13

parties. Eleven days of school left. After today, only ten. Two weeks. Couldn't wait.

But behind that, there lurked another question: Who shoots those cedar arrows?

Maybe I *should* go tree planting, after all.

2 The Ranger Station

"Mom," I said during supper after my last day of school, "I've been thinking about going tree planting with Penny's church's Earthkeepers group."

"I think that would be a good idea," she replied. "Shall I call Uncle Andrew and see whether he'll be up at the cabin then?"

I didn't answer right away and Mom looked up to see what was wrong. "Sure," I said finally. "Just don't plan a lot of things that we end up not doing."

She looked at me quietly for a few seconds, then said, "You haven't forgiven me for two years ago, have you?"

"It's not that. It wasn't your fault. It's just easier to do things as they come up instead of making all these big plans and then being disappointed when they don't work out."

She nodded, then said, "Okay. No promises, then. But I could at least call him, couldn't I? Just to see?"

It took Mom several calls to find out that Uncle Andrew was already on his way up to the cabin from Arizona. He was due there in two or three days. "I'll try calling the cabin every evening until he shows up," she said.

"I thought he had a phone in his car," I said.

"You know, I think you're right. If I could catch him on the road south of here, maybe he'd stop in for a visit on his way north."

I smiled. I hoped he would. I enjoyed having Uncle Andrew around. We always went out to eat—and he sometimes took me to weird stuff like rodeos and tractor pulls.

"Did Penny get any sort of flyer or schedule about the tree planting? If Andy can't stop here, at least I want to be able to tell him exactly when you and Penny will be coming."

Penny had given me a schedule weeks earlier. I ran up to my room and got it. Back in the kitchen, I smoothed it out on the counter in front of Mom and me as if it were a treasure map. Dates, times, campsites—it was all there.

"I've met their youth director," Mom said, "but I can't remember her name."

"Barb."

"You'd better call Barb right now and tell her you want to go along."

Mom came home from the office the next day and announced, "I finally got hold of your Uncle Andrew. He was down in Iowa somewhere and said he'd swing by and spend the night with us. He could be here in the next hour or so."

"Great!"

"It won't be so great," Mom said, "if someone doesn't clean up around here. Check the guest room, will you? And give the upstairs bathroom a once-over? I'll clean up this disaster area we call a kitchen."

Uncle Andrew swept in a half hour later with his loud, happy voice and strong handshake. The first thing he suggested was that we all go down to the Mandarin Garden for Chinese food.

"Why don't you call Penny and see if she can go with us?" Mom suggested.

"A penny's hardly worth bothering with these days," Uncle Andrew chuckled.

"This one is," Mom laughed. "You'll see. She's one in a million."

Penny had already eaten but said she'd meet us there. When she walked up to our table, Uncle Andrew was just telling us how glad he'd be to get back into the quiet of the north woods.

"It hasn't been so quiet up there lately," Penny said.

"Meaning what?" he asked, standing to shake her hand and be introduced.

Mom and I hadn't told him yet about the kidnapping. We all started talking at once until Mom took over and told the whole story about the kidnapping and the shooting.

"You know," he said thoughtfully, "I remember when that dog was shot. It seemed mysterious at the time—but when you add this one to it, and considering it was a kidnapper this time—I mean, a man and not a dog—well, we're into some pretty interesting stuff."

After dinner, we dropped Penny off at her house, then went home and had a long talk before bedtime. Next morning, Uncle Andrew got up early, made French toast and sausage for Mom before she left for work, and then he and I sat down and ate breakfast together.

"Miss your dad?" he asked after a long silence.

Usually it was hard to talk about that, but with Uncle Andrew it wasn't so bad. "I guess I do. But it's been so long I hardly remember him."

"Maybe you just miss *having* a dad."

"Maybe."

"I wish I could do something about that. I wish I could get him to come back—but it may already be too late for that." He chuckled. "I never could talk him into anything, anyway."

"Sometimes—" I hesitated, then blurted it out before I had a chance to think about how embarrassing a thing it was to say. "Sometimes I wish *you* were my dad."

He smiled. "I wish that, too—a lot. I also wish I had met your mom before my brother did. But—by now we've become too much like brother and sister." I think he said that to keep my imagination from running wild. And from the tone of his voice, I knew he didn't intend to talk anymore about that.

We cleaned up the kitchen, and then he went up to get his things from the guest room. When he came back to the kitchen, he laid his toilet kit and his jacket on the table and gave me a hug.

"You're a good kid, Chad—and your mom's a good woman. My brother ought to be horsewhipped."

Tears formed in my eyes. No, I didn't want my father horsewhipped. I didn't even want a *horse* horse-whipped! But I truly did wish my dad was as kind as Uncle Andrew.

When he saw my tears, he rubbed them away from the corners of my eyes with his two rough thumbs. "I'm leaving now. You and Penny check in with me the minute you get up into my woods—okay?"

"Okay," I said. We shook hands. I could see now why people sometimes shook hands rather than hugged. It was to keep from crying.

Two weeks later we were on our way north. There were six of us in Barb's van: Barb, Penny and I, Jeff, Jenny, and Amy. I didn't know any of the others very well. Jeff belonged to Penny's church but went to a private school in Wisconsin. Jenny and Amy were best friends and were in our grade, but I hardly knew either of them.

Even before the trip was over, we were having fun. We stopped for lunch at a bakery in Hinkley that Uncle Andrew had told us about. After lunch we made a quick trip through the museum that told all about the great Hinkley forest fire.

Two hours later, just a mile or two north of Marcell, we stopped at a forest-ranger station. A ranger named Marsha took us all into a conference room, spread three large Itasca National Forest maps on the table so all of us could see, and then showed us the site that needed replanting.

"Where was the shooting?" Jeff asked in a whisper.

"I was hoping you wouldn't bring that up," the ranger said. She was young with reddish hair. Her soft green eyes almost matched her uniform. She shrugged, then put her finger down on the map. "Right here."

"That close?" Jeff said excitedly.

"That close," Marsha, the ranger, said. "We've had several meetings about it, and we've had our rangers in that area looking around. But we haven't seen a thing and we're expecting no more trouble. While you're working, we'll have a ranger checking on you every hour or so. And we're giving your advisor— it's Barb, isn't it?" she asked, turning to Barb. Barb nodded. "We're giving Barb a two-way radio so she can instantly contact either our office or the Itasca County Sheriff's office. You should have no problems." She stood up from the table, looked around the group, and then asked, "Any questions?"

Silence. "Just one," Barb said. "When do we start?"

"At eight o'clock sharp tomorrow morning. Come here first and we'll take you to the site. After that, you'll be able to find your way there on your own."

When we filed out of the conference room, Uncle Andrew was standing in the lobby chatting with one of the rangers. Marsha greeted him warmly, "Hey, Andy, you're back."

"Sure am—and I've got an idea for this group. I know you have them scheduled to camp at Walking Bear Campground, but since they haven't unpacked yet, how about they spend their first night camping at my place? And their last night, too, if they want, so we can have a big cookout or something."

"I have no problem with that," the ranger said, turning to Barb and raising an eyebrow as if to say, "What about you?"

"Fine with me," Barb said. Penny had told me about how Barb could make the unexpected—like a car breaking down or a heavy rainstorm—seem like a neat adventure. On one rainy campout they had cut slits in garbage bags, pulled them over their heads like ponchos, and then played a bunch of crazy games in the rain.

We piled back into Barb's van while Uncle Andrew and Barb stood off to the side having a conference —probably about supper. Then Barb climbed behind the wheel, and we backtracked a couple of miles from the ranger station to Marcell, where our whole gang swarmed through the Frontier Store. We bought junk food and souvenirs while Barb picked up a few groceries and Uncle Andrew bought a plastic bag of minnows for fishing. Finally we were on our way to Horseshoe Lake.

I hadn't been to Uncle Andrew's cabin in four or five years. I could barely remember it when we drove in off the winding dirt road. We all piled out of the van and stood in a circle for a little meeting.

"My land goes as far that way as that tall red pine," Uncle Andrew said, pointing, "and as far that way as the fence. Up over the hill behind us is a swamp, and of course, down the hill is the lakeshore. Use the buddy system if you want to take a swim. Anyone out in the boat or the canoe absolutely has to wear a life jacket. Stay in sight of the dock so we can call you when supper's ready. When shall we eat, Barb?"

"As late as possible," Jeff said. "I want to go canoeing."

"It's 6:00 now," Barb said, looking at her watch. "How about 8:30?"

"Fine," Uncle Andrew said.

The rest of us nodded or grunted and then took off down the hill toward the lake.

Singing to Mr. Archer

Barb nearly went nuts trying to get us off the lake in time for supper. Jeff and I were in the canoe. Penny, Amy, and Jenny were out in the boat. Jenny kept slipping out of her life jacket and jumping out of the boat, rocking it, and scaring Amy—who was wearing *two* life jackets, just in case. Amy screamed and laughed every time the boat rocked.

Before we had gone out in the canoe, Jeff and I had waded along the shore in the shallow water and gathered half a bucket of clams. After Barb called us in, Jeff reached down into the bucket of water and pulled one out. "Are these any good to eat?" he asked.

"I don't know," Barb answered, "but Chad's Uncle Andrew will. For now, why don't you just empty the bucket into the lake right there under the dock."

"Let them go?"

"They're clams." Barb nudged him playfully with the toe of her tennis shoe. "Not fish. They won't swim away. They'll be there tomorrow—probably even Friday when we come back. If they're good to eat, we'll have a clambake on Friday. Fair enough?"

Jeff and I nodded.

"Besides, if you leave them in the bucket," Barb warned, "they might all die."

Then she sent the girls and Jeff up the hill to help Uncle Andrew at the cabin while Penny and I stayed to help her put the boating gear away.

When we got up to the cabin, Uncle Andrew already had a campfire going out in back. He had set logs in a circle around the fire so we all could sit. We held hands and prayed. Barb reminded us to be thankful—and to be good to each other as we traveled and worked together. She thanked God for my Uncle Andrew, too. I sure agreed with that. I silently prayed for my father. I wasn't exactly thankful for him, but I prayed for him anyway.

During the silent prayer, I prayed for the "good guy" of the forest, Mr. Archer, whoever he was. I asked God to protect us all in the woods. And if Mr. Archer happened to be a *bad* guy—I mean, who knows, he could turn out to be an escaped convict or something—that God would protect us from him, too.

After the prayer, our little group got back to talking and laughing. Jeff asked whether we could eat the clams.

"The lake likes them better than you would," Uncle Andrew said. "They're good for the lake. They help keep the water clean. You did just the right thing by leaving them under the dock. The fish from this lake taste a lot better—but if you want to try to fry up a couple of clams, I'll show you how on Friday."

We cooked our bratwurst over the fire and ate and laughed and talked. Then Barb and Uncle Andrew went into the cabin and came back with graham crackers, marshmallows, and chocolate bars.

"S'mores," Uncle Andrew announced, then he showed us how to make them.

"How come they call them 'S'mores'?" Jeff asked.

"Because," Barb explained, "when you eat one, you always say, 'I want s'more.'"

Everyone laughed and got busy making S'mores.

"It'll be dark in about an hour," Barb said. "Time to set up your tents and bedrolls. Tomorrow morning, it's up at 6:30." Everyone groaned. "The minute you get up tomorrow morning, pack your things—everything, tents and all. We'll eat and try to be on our way by 7:45." More groans. "Remember," she said, in a funny 'Mister Rogers' voice, "we came up here to plant trees. Trees are our friends. They put moisture into the air—and oxygen, too. Tree planters are God's little helpers." She put an index finger gently on the tip of Amy's nose as she said it. "We're going to put in a good four days' work," Barb went on. "Then we'll come back here and stay over on Friday night to celebrate. Okay?"

Sounded okay to everyone. Jenny and Barb set up their tent below the hill by the swamp. Penny and Amy decided just to roll out their sleeping bags on the rug inside the cabin—probably so that Amy wouldn't have to worry about bears. Penny said she was sleeping inside so she wouldn't have to repack a tent.

Jeff and I set up our tent just outside the campfire ring so we could watch the fire die out through the tent flap. "Jeff's okay," I decided, "even if he does go to a private school."

I slept fine, considering I was sleeping on the ground. I had a strange dream, though, about the man who shot the arrows. Penny had called him "Robin Hood" when we first read the story in the paper. In my dream, he was dressed all in green, except for his bow, which was silver and shiny. He was holding on to one of my legs. I was dragging him along. It didn't seem like I was trying to get away. More like he needed help. I didn't even know if I could help him. The dream woke me up. Wide awake, I pulled back the tent flap and looked around. The campfire was nothing but a few glowing embers. The stars were beautiful.

At almost exactly 7:45, we were all seat-belted into the van and driving the five miles back to the ranger station. Marsha came out to meet the van. "Follow us," she said, pointing to their pickup. "It's about four miles from here. This is Don." She pointed to the ranger beside her. We all said hi. "Anyone want to ride with Don and me?"

Jeff and Penny and I ran for the pickup truck. We slipped into the bench seat in the back of the cab. I looked out the back window. Sitting in the bed of the truck were buckets of baby trees and a half-dozen, weird-looking, shovel-like tools. A plastic tank of water on a trailer was hooked behind the truck. We were in for a day's work, I could see that.

When we got to the clearing where we were to plant trees, we helped unhook the water tank trailer and unload the tools and trees. Then Don demonstrated tree planting. He held up one of the shovel-like tools. It looked like a wedge with a footrest and a T-handle. He called it a "dibble."

"You push it into the ground with your foot," he said, "like this. Then you separate out one seedling tree—just one. You put it in this deep," he showed us, "pour the hole full of water, then you push the dibble into the ground about this far away and wedge the dirt back against the seedling."

It looked simple.

"The seedlings have to stay in the bucket of water until just before they go into the ground. If the roots ever dry out, they'll die."

"No use planting dead trees," Marsha added, smiling.

They showed us how to space the trees; then the two of them handed out to each pair of us a tool and a pail of seedlings and a bucket for water. Jeff looked like he wanted to pair up with me, but Barb took his arm. Amy latched onto Jenny, so Penny and I got to plant together.

"Don and I have to check for wind damage along a few miles of power line," Marsha said before she and Don drove off in the Forest Service truck. "We'll check in with you about 10:00," she added, "and again before we break for lunch."

We began planting trees slowly at first, but as we went we picked up speed. Pretty soon we were all working at a fast pace, like old pros. We stopped about 9:30 to eat trail mix and drink apple juice.

"Wonder if Mr. Archer is watching us," Penny whispered, staring out into the woods with an X-ray-vision gaze.

"If he is, I don't think we'd ever know it," I whispered back. "He's lived in these woods for at least two years, and no one's ever seen him. Not even the rangers know where he is."

"Wish I could see him and talk to him. He saved my Aunt Jean."

As we sat there crunching on our nuts and raisins and sipping apple juice from paper cups, Penny quietly stood up. "Mr. Archer," she said to the woods softly. Then louder, "*Mr. Archer!*"

"Is she nuts, or what?" Jeff laughed. "Who's Mr. Archer?"

"Planted too many trees," Jenny suggested.

"Who you talking to, Penny?" Barb asked.

"I was just thinking of the man with the bow and arrow, the one who helped my Aunt Jean. Maybe he's watching us."

Amy shuddered.

"I just want to say hello to him," Penny said softly, "and thank him."

Then she called out again, and before anyone could say anything, Jeff had taken it up. "Hello, Mr. Archer!" he shouted. Then Jenny joined in: "Hello, Mr. Archer!"

Pretty soon Barb and I and even Amy joined in. We chanted and laughed as if we were being led by a cheerleader and were at one of our school games. But Penny stopped yelling and just watched the rest of us. I stopped to watch her.

"Maybe it's not funny," she said when the rest finally quieted down. "Maybe it's not so great being out here in the woods all by yourself."

"I wouldn't mind," Jeff said, smiling. "Wouldn't have to go back to school."

"Well, if he's out there," Penny said, "I just want to say hello. I don't want him to think we're making fun of him."

"We're not *making* fun, Penny," Barb said gently. "We're just *having* fun. Anyway," she said, standing, "it's time we quit yelling at the woods and get back to work."

No one said anything else about the archer until late in the afternoon, when Jenny started humming "Old MacDonald Had a Farm." Before long she was making up verses about Mr. Archer:

Mr. Archer had a woods,
Ee-eye, ee-eye oh.
And in this woods he had a bear,
Ee-eye, ee-eye oh.
With a growl, growl here, And a growl, growl there,
Here a growl, there a growl, Everywhere a growl, growl,
Mr. Archer had a woods,
Ee-eye, ee-eye oh.

Singing made the hard work seem easier, so we all enjoyed it—even Penny. I was watching her especially. We made up verses about deer and rabbits and eagles and grouse. When we got to porcupine, no one knew what sound a porcupine made, not even Barb. Finally Jeff shouted, "It's a pork, isn't it? *Pork*-upine? A pig *oinks*." Everyone laughed and sang:

With an oink, oink here,
And an oink, oink there . . .

When we ran out of wild forest animals to sing about, it was quiet for a few moments, then Jenny sang:

Mr. Archer had a woods,
Ee-eye, ee-eye, oh.
And in this woods he had a bow,
Ee-eye, ee-eye, oh.
With a shoot, shoot here . . .

Everyone joined in the chorus. But I watched Penny carefully as Jenny went on to the next verse:

Mr. Archer had a woods,
Ee-eye, ee-eye, oh.
And to this woods there came Aunt Jean,
Ee-eye, ee-eye, oh.
With a "No no!" here, And a "No no!" there . . .

Barb glanced quickly at Penny and said, "That's enough, Jenny. Penny's Aunt Jean was lucky. Not every kidnapped woman is that lucky. It could have ended very differently."

We worked quietly for a while, until Barb started us on some camp songs. About 4:30, Barb decided we should quit. "Take your dibble and make a hole where your next tree will be planted. Put a stick or some other marker in the hole. Then tomorrow morning, we'll all know where to start. Put your tools on the trailer and your buckets of trees underneath, in the shade. The minute we get back to camp, we'll go for a swim. Then I want three volunteers to help with supper."

Penny and I marked our place, but before we headed back to the trailer to put our gear away, she stopped for a minute and stared into the woods. "What's wrong?" I asked.

"I just couldn't help thinking of my Aunt Jean," she said, "being dragged up here into the woods and scared half to death—and Mr. Archer, who had to shoot someone to save her."

"Yeah," I said, not knowing what else to say.

"Thank God he was here," Penny added.

She smiled softly then, and slugged me in the shoulder. We walked over and put our trees and tools away.

4 Exchanging Gifts

We drove to the forest camp, took a swim, pitched our tents, and built a fire. Between tree planting and setting up camp, none of us had much energy left for running around that night—and anyway, Barb set a strict bedtime so we could all get some sleep. A hot supper tasted wonderful after working all day, and the swim felt good, too. One nice thing about being in the water—there were no mosquitoes.

The next morning we packed our snacks and lunch and piled into the van for Tree Planting, Day Two. When we got to the site, Marsha and Don were in their ranger truck, waiting for us. We gathered in a group to listen.

"Don and I have already walked the area this morning," Marsha said, "and we think you did a great job yesterday. We really appreciate the careful work you're doing—and the amount you're getting done. We have no added instructions—except to ask you to be a little more careful about your spacing of trees. It looks like the pairs of you are spacing your own trees just fine, but you aren't always noticing where your friends are planting. Oh, and yes," she added with a playful smile. "It's nice to try to bring a little beauty into your work space, but the Forest Service tends to frown on the transplanting of wildflowers."

I didn't know what she meant by that, and from the looks on their faces, neither did anyone else. Penny and I were the first ones out into the clearing, ready to get back to planting. When we got to our marker, Penny gasped, "Look!" She dropped to her knees and touched the base of our marker stick. There were five little wildflowers planted around the base of our stick. So that's what Marsha had meant. She thought we'd planted the flowers.

"It's him," Penny whispered.

"Who?"

"Mr. Archer."

"How do you know?"

"I just know."

"I wonder if he planted flowers around all the markers."

"Let's go look," Penny whispered.

We hurried off in two directions, talking with the others and sneaking quick looks at their markers. When we came back I asked, "Did you find any?"

"No," Penny said.

"Neither did I. It was for you, then," I said. "Mr. Archer planted them for you. Do you know what that means?"

"No," Penny said, back on her knees and touching the flowers gently with her fingers.

"It means he *was* in the woods yesterday, watching everything we did and listening to everything we said. He heard you calling to him, and telling the rest of us that it wasn't funny—sticking up for him."

"Do you think so?"

"These flowers are his way of thanking you. He didn't put flowers on anybody else's marker. Hey!" I shouted to the others, about to call them over.

"Don't tell!" Penny hissed, grabbing my arm.

"Uh—hey," I said, quickly changing my message. "Let's count how many trees each team plants today—like a contest."

"Thanks," Penny whispered.

Everyone stopped and looked at Barb. I could see her running that one over in her mind. "Not a contest," she finally said. "If we try to plant too fast, just to win a contest, we might do careless work. I'll come up with a different contest—maybe I'll write down two numbers of trees planted, and whoever comes closest to those numbers today will win a prize."

"What are the prizes?" Jeff asked.

"Something good to eat," Barb grinned.

"Yum!" Jenny shouted. Things quieted down then, and we all went to work.

"He's out there," Penny whispered as she pushed the dibble into the sandy earth. "Now I know for sure. I was half kidding yesterday, but now I'm convinced. He's there. He can see us, and he can hear us."

"So what do we do?"

"Nothing," Penny said, pushing the earth back against the seedling I had put in the hole. "At least not now."

"We could come over here the day after we finish," I said, "after the others go back, when just the two of us are staying with my uncle."

Penny nodded. "And we could leave a note for Mr. Archer and tell him so."

Every now and then, throughout the day, Penny would look off into the woods and kind of half wave and smile. Then when we had finished for the day, and were putting our marker stick at the end of the row, Penny reached behind her head and untied the little purple ribbon she was wearing on her braid.

"I'm going to tie this onto our marker stick as a 'thank you' for the flowers," she said.

"Let's leave him some trail mix, too," I whispered.

We each had a plastic bag of it in our pocket, each bag about half full. We combined both bags of nuts and dried fruit into one, then put one bag inside the other. Penny tied the ribbon to the trail mix, then tied them both to our marker stick.

At the end of the day, Barb and Jeff won one of Barb's prizes, and Jenny and Amy won the other. Since Penny and I were the only ones who didn't win, Barb gave us a prize, too. Each pair of us got a bag of gummi bears.

That night by the campfire, Penny and I talked about other things we could leave for Mr. Archer if he took the trail mix we left for him. "Let's take him a can of pop and a candy bar," I said. "I'll bet he hasn't had anything like that for a long time."

"What does he need?" Penny asked. "I mean, what would someone living alone in the woods really need?" We both thought for a long time and then Penny said, "I think I'll give him a toothbrush and toothpaste."

"Yuck," I said. "Not even a hermit would want to use someone else's toothbrush."

"Not mine, dummy. I have a new one in my bag. It's still in the box. I don't have extra toothpaste, though. I'll have to give him mine."

When we got back to the work site the next morning, the trail mix was gone and so was the purple ribbon. I looked to see if Mr. Archer had left anything for us as a message, but I didn't see anything. Just when I was beginning to think that maybe the whole deal was a daydream and that some forest animal or bird had carried away our trail mix and feasted on it, Penny saw the leather thong wrapped around our stick. It was about as thin as a piece of spaghetti and almost as soft. It was dyed a soft red, and it seemed to be buckskin.

"Do you mind if I have it?" Penny asked, running the thong through her fingers.

"He probably left it for you," I said.

Penny reached back, then, and tied the thong on top of the rubber band she had wrapped around her braid after breakfast. When she had finished tying it, she turned toward the woods, raised her hand above her head, and waved it back and forth, turning as she waved, like an actress bowing to all sections of her audience.

Jeff saw her waving. He looked at me and drew circles around his ear with his forefinger, then pointed at Penny, raising his eyebrows. Then he shook his head and went back to work.

That night we left pop, two candy bars, toothpaste, and a toothbrush for the hidden archer. The pop can was too big to go into the dibble hole, so I laid it on top of the other things to cover them.

The next morning we brought all sorts of things to give to Mr. Archer: soap, a little bottle of aspirin, a container of dental floss—which he could use for thread or string if he didn't want to use it on his teeth—and a plastic bag full of coffee we sneaked out of Barb's can in the food locker.

It was Friday, our last day of tree planting. I could see Penny starting to get nervous and fidgety. She wanted to meet Mr. Archer.

We hurried to our marker stick to see if he had left anything. At first I didn't see anything; then we spotted two loops of thong tucked into the grass around the bottom of the stick. I lifted the stick out of the hole and Penny bent over and picked up the thongs. When she pulled them up out of the dibble hole we could see they were two identical necklaces. Each had a tooth on it, a wide and very sharp tooth.

"These teeth look like they came from Krissy down the block," Penny said.

"You mean the girl the kids call Beaver?"

"That's what they are," Penny said. "Beaver teeth." She handed me one of the necklaces and we each put one on.

"Maybe he gave us teeth to thank you for the *tooth*brush," I said.

We fiddled with our necklaces, then looked at each other's. Penny again raised her hand and turned to the woods all around and waved thanks. This time I did, too.

Jeff saw us. He drew circles around both his ears, laughed, and pointed at the two of us. "You're both nuts," he shouted.

40

About 4:30, Marsha and Don drove in to thank us and to pick up the tools. Each team finished the row it was planting. Since we all knew we wouldn't be back, no one left markers—no one, that is, except Penny and me. We left a marker so Mr. Archer could find the things we had brought for him—although he probably would have found anything we left, marker or no marker.

Penny and I were still hoping we could come back alone, just the two of us. We had already talked to Uncle Andrew about driving us out here the day after the others left. We told him we wanted to plant more trees—but we didn't tell him that that was just to have something to do while we waited for Mr. Archer.

I had this feeling that if we came back, just the two of us, maybe Penny would get her wish—Mr. Archer would come out of the woods. If he would come out for anyone, he would do it for Penny. It was obvious that he liked her.

Penny left a note with the things:

OUR GROUP ISN'T COMING BACK.
BUT WE WILL TRY TO COME BACK,
JUST THE TWO OF US.
I'M PENNY AND HE'S CHAD.
THANKS FOR THE NECKLACES.
AND THANKS FOR SAVING MY AUNT JEAN
WITH YOUR ARROW.

When Marsha and Don looked across the clearing, she couldn't believe it. "We had another group scheduled in here for next week," she said, "but you guys have done so well there are only a few hours of work left here."

"We could do it," Penny said, without even asking me. "Chad and I."

"They're staying a couple of extra days with Chad's Uncle Andrew," Barb explained.

"You really want to?" Marsha asked.

"Sure," Penny insisted.

"You, too?" Marsha turned to me.

"Yeah."

"Well, I'll plan on you starting a little later tomorrow," Marsha said. "If you stay up tonight singing songs with these night owls, and then have to say all your good-byes in the morning, you won't want to be here at 8:00."

"That's for sure," Barb said, nodding to the two of us.

"How about 10:00?" Marsha asked. Penny and I nodded.

"Will Andy give you a ride, or should we pick you up?" Don asked.

"He'll give us a ride," I said. "And if he can't, we'll call."

Before we all piled into Barb's van for the last time, Jeff turned to the others and said, "Let's say good-bye to Penny's friend in the woods. Let's all shout together, 'Good-bye, Mr. Archer.'"

He directed with his hands, and all of us shouted at the top of our lungs: "*Good-bye, Mr. Archer!*"

Jeff put his finger to his lips for silence, then cupped his ear as if to listen for an answer.

From what seemed like miles away, we heard what sounded like the call of a wolf: "*Ow-oooooooooooo.*"

"Wow!" Penny shuddered. She whispered to me so no one else would hear. "He answered!"

5 Tomorrow

On Friday night at Uncle Andrew's, we all played capture-the-flag and hide-and-seek. Even Uncle Andrew—although sometimes he was puffing so hard he had to sit down. Afterward we all roasted hot dogs over the fire and made S'mores. Everyone had a great time, including Penny. There were moments, though, when she seemed far away, like she wasn't thinking about what she was doing. I was sure her mind was on Mr. Archer.

After supper, Uncle Andrew took Jeff and Jenny and Barb fishing. They came back with two bass and three northern pike. "I'll fry you some fish for breakfast," he said.

The next morning we ate what Uncle Andrew called "a real cabin breakfast": oatmeal and fried fish and bacon and sausage and eggs and toast and juice and milk—and for Barb and Uncle Andrew, coffee. Penny and I both heard Barb wonder out loud where all her own coffee had gone. We just smiled at each other. I was sure that Barb would have offered to give Mr. Archer coffee if we had dared tell her what we were doing. As I watched her and my uncle sipping coffee and chatting, I hoped that Mr. Archer was enjoying his coffee as much as they were. *And, Lord, bring him someone to talk to, too,* I prayed silently, *so he doesn't have to be lonely. Somebody like Penny and me. Maybe today. Maybe.*

Everyone packed stuff into Barb's van, we said our good-byes, and they were gone. I had learned to like them all—Jeff and Jenny and Amy and especially Barb. I knew I'd see Jenny and Amy when school started, but I didn't know if I'd ever see Jeff again. It might have been a sadder good-bye if Penny and I hadn't been so excited about going back to find Mr. Archer.

Uncle Andrew said he'd be glad to drive us to the ranger station. His plan was to spend the day with us, and he said so as we were packing our lunches.

"You don't need to do that," Penny said. "We'll be all right. He wouldn't hurt us."

"He?" Uncle Andrew said. "Oh. You mean the bow-and-arrow man. I agree. I think he's a helper, not a hurter. No, the only critter I ever worry about is moose. When they're mating, they can get mean."

"How about bear?" I asked, remembering the tracks.

"We only have black bear around here. They'll mess up your campsite and eat your food, but there's no record of a black bear ever hurting anyone here in Minnesota. They like to bluff, but if you stand your ground, or shout, or bang pans together, they'll turn and run."

"We'll be okay, Uncle Andrew, honest," Penny pleaded. She must have thought, as I did, that our best chance to meet Mr. Archer was for us to be alone.

"Maybe we could use the same walkie-talkie Barb had," I suggested.

"Of course," Penny said. "Then if we needed help, we could call either the Forest Service or the sheriff."

"Well, maybe." Uncle Andrew still seemed uneasy. "We'll see what Marsha and the others at the ranger station have to say. If they think it'll be safe, then it's all right with me."

We talked everyone into it. At the ranger station, Marsha gave us the communicator—along with a brief lesson. "Don't move this dial, though," she warned, pointing to it. "It sets the frequency, and it's very hard to reset out in the woods. We usually have to bring these things back to the station to get them reset."

We promised not to touch it. We would have promised almost anything to be left alone in that clearing.

"We pulled our water trailer out of there yesterday," Marsha said. "It was almost empty. We'll take a few five-gallon pails of water with us. That should be enough to finish up."

A half hour later we were at the planting site. We unloaded water and trees; then Marsha checked in with the station to see if the communicator was working. "Now you try it," she said to Penny and me. We did. It was simple—or seemed to be.

After they left, Penny and I just sat down and talked. "How are we going to do this?" Penny asked.

"I don't know," I answered. "Maybe just be honest. Tell him we want to talk with him. Tell him we want to thank him."

That's what we did. We began to plant trees, and about every ten trees or so, Penny would stand up and

47

shout to the woods, "Please, Mr. Archer. Come out and talk with us."

The morning went by without any response from anyone except the crows and ravens that flew overhead. The ravens made especially spooky sounds. I was beginning to think coming out into the woods all alone hadn't been such a great idea.

Penny just seemed to be getting impatient. Again and again during the morning, she tried to talk with Mr. Archer. By afternoon, she was pleading with him: "Come out and talk!" she shouted. "Please!" She mentioned her Aunt Jean over and over again and promised that we wouldn't tell anyone. She told him how urgent it was— that we only had two more days.

Uncle Andrew was due at 4:00.

Finally, sometime after 3:30, Penny stood up, cupped her hands around her mouth, and shouted, "I give up!"

It was deathly silent for a minute or two more— then I heard a swish, and then a *thunk*. The *thunk* sound came from down by my feet. I looked down and there was an arrow—a home-made looking arrow, like the ones we had read about in the newspaper.

Penny didn't see it. I bent down and picked it up. For a tip, it just had a lead fishing sinker lashed on with fishing line. The arrow was blunt—obviously not made to kill anything. And tied to the shaft was a flower—tied with Penny's purple ribbon!

"Look," I whispered to Penny, dropping to my knees and laying the arrow down in front of her.

"Oh," she said softly, holding the arrow in front of her as a smile spread slowly across her face. She looked out into the woods and shouted, "Thank you," untying the flower and sticking it into her hair. She kneeled down and laid the ribbon in front of her without taking her eyes off the woods. "Come out now," she shouted. "We haven't much time. Uncle Andrew will be back in just a few minutes."

I picked up the ribbon and ran it through my fingers as she shouted—until suddenly I noticed a word carefully written on the ribbon in charcoal: "TOMORROW."

"Look," I said to Penny.

"Tomorrow," she mouthed silently. Then aloud to me, "Tomorrow." Then she shouted to the woods, "Tomorrow. Yes. Tomorrow. We'll be back tomorrow morning. You'll come out then and we'll talk. Tomorrow. For sure. Tomorrow."

Just then Uncle Andrew's car wheeled in. Penny hid the wooden arrow behind her back and kept it there until she was able to get to her backpack and slip it in. I carried our dibble and pail of seedlings back to the car.

"Marsha said if you were going to come back tomorrow, you should just leave the tools and stuff here under a bush."

"We're coming back tomorrow," I said, "for sure!"

We found a bush and put the dibble and the pail of seedlings under it. The buckets of water we left by the road, right where they had been unloaded. "No sense moving them," Uncle Andrew said.

When Penny walked up with her flower in her hair, Uncle Andrew said, "Looks nice."

Penny smiled.

That night, Uncle Andrew took us fishing. It was calm and beautiful on the lake, and we watched most of the sunset. The electric trolling motor hummed quietly, and I watched Uncle Andrew's profile as, one hand on the motor, he guided us just where he wanted us to go. I found myself wondering why, growing up in the same home, my dad and Uncle Andrew had turned out so differently. Why couldn't I have a dad like Uncle Andrew, or like some of the other guys have?

When we'd been fishing for about a half hour, Penny hooked a fish. Uncle Andrew took her rod and felt it for a moment and then handed it back. "Northern pike," he said. "Good-sized. A lunker. That one fish, if we land him, will be enough to feed all of us. Enough even for your mom if she should come early," he said to me, "and leftovers besides."

"What do I do?" Penny asked excitedly.

"Not much when he's pulling line out like that. Just keep your rod tip up and let him work against the spring of the rod. Never point your rod at the fish. He'll break the line, then. Once he stops, you'll have to pump him in."

"How do I do that?"

Uncle Andrew took her rod and said, "Watch." He first raised the rod tip slowly, drawing the fish in. Then as he slowly lowered the rod, he wound the reel, taking in line. "You pull the fish in with the rod, not the reel," he said. "First you lift the fish with the rod, then you reel in line with the reel. Also, you have to keep the line tight all the time or he'll spit out the hook."

He handed Penny the rod again, then reached both arms around her and showed her how. "Now. Slowly lift up on your rod. That brings the fish closer to the boat. Then reel in line as you lower the rod tip again. Then you do it again. Lift up and reel in. Lift up and reel in. That's 'pumping.'" He leaned back and let her try it herself.

We both watched as Penny sat in the middle of the boat and pumped in her fish. When he was about twenty yards from the boat, he jumped.

"They don't do that very often, northerns don't," Uncle Andrew said. "Fun, isn't it?"

"Yeah," Penny gasped, out of breath.

Suddenly her line went slack.

"Is he gone?" Uncle Andrew asked.

"I don't know," Penny answered.

"Maybe he's running in. Stand up," Uncle Andrew told her hurriedly, "lift your rod as high as you can and reel in the line as fast as you can." Uncle Andrew leaned forward and put both hands on Penny's waist to steady her as she stood up in the center of the boat. Her hands and the handle of the fishing rod were now way above her head. She was holding the rod high and reeling in line fast. Suddenly the line went taut again.

"Hooray!" Uncle Andrew shouted. "He's still there."

Penny played her fish for several more minutes before she was able to bring him alongside the boat. Then Uncle Andrew netted him. He lifted the net and the fish over the side and into the boat, then took the fish out of the net. He removed the hook and held him up. "Shall we let him go?" he asked with a wry smile on his face.

"No!" Penny shouted. "It's the only fish I've ever caught!"

Uncle Andrew nodded. "It's hard to put a fish back sometimes, especially a big fish or a trophy fish. Sometimes 'catch and release' is the best way, though, even though some of the fish we release die. Still, nothing is wasted—sickly fish are eaten by bigger fish, or eagles, or ospreys. If they die, crawfish and turtles eat them."

He held Penny's fish up again. "I think we can keep this one. There are a lot of fish this size in this lake, and plenty of breeders."

"Yay!" Penny shouted, whipping her pole around and snapping the hooks dangerously through the air.

"Careful," Uncle Andrew warned. "You don't want to hook someone else in the boat."

As he was putting the big northern on the stringer, Uncle Andrew turned the fish's mouth toward us and showed us his teeth. "Those teeth are sharp as razors. If you're unlucky enough to get your hand in his mouth, you'll get a dozen slits as neat as if they were made by a doctor's scalpel."

"Let's catch another one," Penny puffed, still out of breath.

"My idea was to catch enough to eat," Uncle Andrew said, "and then quit fishing. We've already done that."

"We can't quit now," Penny pleaded.

"I guess not," he chuckled. "Maybe Chad will catch the next one."

We fished for another hour. Uncle Andrew and I caught a couple of smaller northerns and he caught a nice bass. We kept the bass and released the northerns.

As we turned back toward the cabin, I was feeling kind of grumpy and couldn't figure out why—until I realized I was jealous of Penny and her big fish.

When we got back to the cabin, Uncle Andrew wanted to take pictures. "Hold up your fish," he said to Penny.

Penny grabbed the stringer chain with her northern and Uncle Andrew's bass on it, but it was too heavy for her to hold up.

"Help me," Penny said. I grabbed the chain near her hand and helped her lift. "Our fish," she said, nudging me with her elbow and offering me a gentle smile as together we held the fish in front of us.

I smiled back.

There was a flash, and our northern-pike smiles were captured forever on film.

Pleased to Meet You, Mr. Archer

We decided to go back to the clearing earlier the next morning. Uncle Andrew drove us to the ranger station to get the communicator and then dropped us off at the tree-planting area about 8:30. He didn't even get out of the car. "I'll check back with you about noon," he said, and then drove away.

Penny and I looked behind the bush where we had put our dibble and our bucket of seedlings—and they were gone.

"Would he have taken them?" I asked.

We looked out across the planting site. I didn't notice anything different. And then Penny pointed and shouted, "Look!"

Way on the far side of the clearing, so far you could barely see it, was our dibble, stuck into the ground. Beside it was the bucket.

We ran over there, careful not to crush any of the trees we had all planted.

When we got there, Penny picked up the bucket and said, "It's empty. The trees are all gone."

We looked at each other, bewildered, and then looked around—and realized where all the trees had gone. He had planted them. Every one. Mr. Archer had planted the rest of the trees. The whole site was planted. He must have worked until sundown to get it all done. We walked around in different directions, looking at the trees he had planted. Then suddenly I noticed something else—something that made me shiver. "Do you see the tracks?" I shouted.

"I do," Penny called back. "Are they bear tracks?"

"I think so," I said, with a quick look around at the woods.

She came over to me then and we walked around together, studying the tracks. This place seemed pretty spooky all of a sudden, and we looked around us at the woods often.

"Do you think he has a pet bear?" Penny asked.

"I don't know. Maybe the bear came through here later."

"But there were also bear tracks when my Aunt Jean was saved, remember? And look—where are Mr. Archer's tracks?"

Penny was right. There were bear tracks all over, but no human tracks except ours.

A tree-planting bear? An archer bear? Not likely. And it sure hadn't been a bear who wrote "tomorrow" on that ribbon.

When we got back to the dibble, I pulled it out of the ground and Penny picked up the pail. We carried them back by the water buckets and set them down. I picked up one of the water buckets. It was empty. So were the others, all but one—which was still about half full.

"He watered them, too," I said.

"Who?" Penny asked with a half smile. "Mr. Archer or the bear?"

We turned a couple of empty water buckets over and sat down on them. "What do we do now?" I asked.

"We wait, I guess," Penny answered.

We just sat there for a few minutes. "This is boring," Penny said. She stood up and shouted, "Thanks for planting our trees, Mr. Archer. Now we have nothing to do this morning but wait for you—will you come out now?"

She waited, but nothing happened, so she went on. "Please come out. We won't tell anyone, cross our hearts." She crossed her heart and then nodded to me. I stood up and crossed my heart, too. "I've been praying for you, too, Mr. Archer, and I'll keep on praying for you. But it would be a lot easier if I knew what you looked like."

That must have got him, because we heard a rustle across the clearing and then he stepped out. I had never seen anything like him before, except maybe on TV. He had shoulder-length hair and a shaggy beard, and he was wearing what looked like blue jeans. It was hard to tell because they had so many buckskin patches on them. He wasn't big at all. Just a bit bigger than my mom.

His hat was shaped like a straw hat but seemed to be woven from narrow strips of birch bark. It had a net of strings or vines or something on the sides and in back. They hung down to his shoulders—maybe to help keep the mosquitoes away. *Bug spray,* I thought, remembering the list of things we thought he would need in the woods.

He wore what looked like a buckskin jacket, open at the front. His chest was bare and hairy. He had a tube of birch bark strapped over his shoulder with about a dozen of his homemade cedar arrows in it.

The bow he carried looked completely out of place. It was a compound bow, the kind I'd seen hanging in the sporting-goods sections of department stores. It had pulleys and strings running back and forth—not at all like Robin Hood would have carried—and certainly not homemade like the arrows.

On his belt was a leather pouch, and he wore leather sandals. Also hanging from his belt were what looked like wooden shoes or clogs. He had one hanging on each side, probably so they wouldn't bang together and make noise when he walked.

I saw part of the bottom of one. It had a strange round shape to it. But I was confused—if he had carved shoes for himself, why wasn't he wearing them?

Penny stood up and started to walk toward him. I wasn't sure about this, now that he was right here. I mean, could we trust this man? Does someone who lives alone out in the woods get sort of crazy? Should we trust someone whose arrows had killed a dog and wounded a man? But I couldn't let Penny go out there alone, so I walked along beside her.

When we came near him, she stretched out her right hand. He shifted his bow to his left hand and reached out his right for Penny's hand.

"Hello," he said as they shook hands. His voice was fast and high and hollow. It sounded exactly like the newsreel voices you hear on films that go back to the

Second World War. Had his voice changed from living alone? Did he talk to himself? *Did* he live alone, or was there someone else out here too?

"I'm glad you came out," Penny said. "I'm Penny." She pointed to me and said, "He's Chad." I shook hands with him, too. His hands were rough and his handshake firm.

"Please. Into the woods," he said in his high voice. "There may be airplanes, or helicopters." He pointed to the sky.

"Why don't you want to be seen?" I asked.

He ignored the question as he turned and stepped back into the woods, and Penny shot me a warning glance. Wrong question. I had to be careful.

"I love the necklace," Penny said, trying to set him at ease. She held the necklace out from her chest. "Is that a beaver tooth?" she asked.

"Yes. I didn't kill him, though. Some hunter shot him in the water and then just left him. Made me a nice winter hat. And soup." His chuckle was more like a giggle. "I saved all his teeth."

"Where's your pet bear?" I asked.

He laughed. He reached down to his belt and untied a thong that held one of the wooden shoes. He slipped out of his moccasin and slipped into the wooden shoe—then pressed it into the sand in front of us. When he lifted up the wooden shoe, all we saw under it was a bear track.

He slipped out of the wooden shoe and back into his moccasin. "See?" he said, turning the wooden shoe over for us. "Carved like a bear paw. To fool a real woodsman, though, I'd have to hop."

Penny was laughing. "That is so funny. You fooled everyone."

He laughed with her. "I also have moose hooves. Drives hunters crazy. They follow me all over the woods."

We laughed together; then there was a long pause. "Where do you live?" Penny finally asked.

There was a long pause while he just looked at us. Then, "You already promised not to tell," he said.

We nodded.

"Did you mean it?"

"Of course," Penny insisted.

"You, too?" He looked at me.

"Sure."

"Then I'll show you."

"We have to leave a note for my uncle," I said. "In case he comes back while we're gone."

"Use birch bark," he said, pulling a wrapped piece of charcoal out of his pouch. He handed Penny the charcoal, walked over to a white tree, and peeled off part of the thin outer layer. "Doesn't hurt the tree much," he said, handing it to me.

Penny handed me the charcoal and I wrote:

We have finished with the trees and are exploring the woods. We won't get lost. We'll be back here at three.
Chad.

Writing with charcoal is slow and messy. While I was writing, Penny went and got the dibble. We jammed the dibble into the dirt at the edge of the field near where Uncle Andrew would have to park and tied the note to it with weed stems.

"Let's go, then," Penny said.

We pulled on our backpacks that had our lunches in them, and off we went. I tried to keep track of where we were walking but so much of the woods looked all the same. I watched the sun so I would at least know which direction we were walking.

As we walked, I noticed Mr. Archer pushing on his stomach from time to time, hard, as if he had a stomachache. Once he stopped completely, bent over, and put both hands to his stomach as if he really hurt.

Finally we stopped. "There," he said, pointing to the side of a hill. I couldn't see anything but bushes and trees. "Follow me," he said. He went up to a bush and pulled it back. There was a cave behind it.

We walked inside. It was too dark to see anything; I put my hands out in front of me so I didn't bang into a wall and stepped slowly. While our eyes were getting used to the dark, I could hear him moving around and then blowing. Then I could see that each time he blew, a red ember on the floor glowed more brightly. He pushed something toward it as it glowed—a dry leaf, it looked like. A couple more blows, and the leaf burst into flame. He used that flame to light two lamps made from tin cans with oil or something in them. In their yellow light, the cave looked even more eerie.

In the far corner was what must have been his bed. On top of a huge leaf pile, a patched-up sleeping bag was nestled in furs. A table and a single chair made of branches were lashed together with thongs. Many of the utensils he cooked with were made of empty tin cans. A big one hung from tall poles that stood over the fire pit. He had carved his cup out of wood.

It was cool in the cave. Penny shivered. "I can't build a fire," he said. "Sorry. I only dare build fires at night. Rangers see the smoke. Please—" He waved us further into the cave. "I only have one chair, but please sit. I have berries, and jerky." He handed us a birch-bark bowl full of dark berries. "June berries," he said. He had laid a few strips of dried meat along the edges.

We tried the berries, carefully at first, then ate more. "They're good," Penny said, smiling. The meat was tough, but I managed to bite off a small piece. The more I chewed, the better it tasted. I smiled as I chewed. "Good," I said.

"I smoked it over the fire," he chuckled.

When we'd finished his food, we dug ours out and shared with him. As we ate and talked, he seemed to relax more—or maybe eating our granola bars and candy just reminded him of civilization. Anyway, his voice got lower and his sentences got longer. "This is good," he said. "And thanks for the candy and soda."

"Glad you liked them," I said.

"What's the date?" he asked.

"June 12," Penny said.

"Well," he said, standing up and checking some charcoal marks on the cave wall. "I'm three days off."

"Not bad," Penny said. Then she slipped in a loaded question. "How long have you been keeping that calendar?"

"Over two years," he said.

"Why are you here," she finally blurted out, "living all by yourself?"

He sighed. "It's a long story."

Penny looked at her watch. "It's 2:30," she said. "We have to get back to the clearing. If we come back tomorrow, will you tell us your story?"

He paused, thoughtful, and then said, "I will."

"Good," she said. "We'll be at the clearing tomorrow at 8:30."

"I'll be watching for you," he said. He stood up then, and as he did, the pain came back to his stomach worse than ever. He doubled over and cried out.

Penny and I looked at each other, alarmed, and then Penny asked, "Are you all right?" in a concerned voice.

He straightened back up slowly. "I guess so. Strange pain. Never had it before."

He led us back to the clearing. I watched the route again, hoping to remember it. He stopped twice on the way back because of the pain.

"I'll watch from the woods," he said as we neared the clearing, "until he picks you up."

We thanked him and said good-bye.

As we walked out into the clearing, I remembered how spooky it had felt this morning. Now, I realized, I felt very safe—as if someone was watching over us.

The Second Mile

Uncle Andrew took us bass fishing after supper. He gave us lessons in casting with an open-faced fishing reel, and showed us where bass like to lurk. We cast our lures and plastic worms near weedbeds and around the branches of trees that the beavers had tipped over into the water.

"I have plenty of fish in the freezer," he said, "so this evening it's going to be catch and release, okay?"

We both nodded.

We didn't keep track of how many bass we caught and released—maybe eight or ten. We all caught some, though, and it was fun. Leaning back in the boat, laughing along with Penny and Uncle Andrew when the bass he was releasing flipped its tail as it dove and splattered him with water, I decided that Jesus knew exactly what he was doing when he chose fishermen for his friends.

The next morning, we were out at the clearing at 8:30. "We'll check the trees to make sure they all look like they're doing okay," I told Uncle Andrew, "and then we'll explore some more. If we need anything, I'll just call on the communicator."

"When do you want me to stop back?"

"Maybe 3:00 or so."

"All right. But you call if you have any trouble."

"We will."

We waited until Uncle Andrew was gone and then called out to the woods: "Mr. Archer! We're here!" We called and called—and then we shouted. We finally went over to the edge of the clearing in the direction of his cave and shouted. Nothing.

"He's not here," Penny finally said, giving up and sagging down against a tree trunk.

"He said he'd be here," I said. "And even without a watch, he must know we'd be here by now."

"Do you suppose he might be hurt—or sick?"

"Maybe his stomachache got worse."

Penny nodded. "Do you think we could find the cave by ourselves?"

"We can try."

Starting out was easy, because we remembered just where we'd gone into the woods. But every few hundred yards we had to stop and figure out which way to go. "I think we went that way," I would say.

"No. I think it was that way," Penny would say.

We'd try one way, and if it didn't feel right after a while, we'd backtrack and try the other. We marked each trail carefully with birch twigs so we could find our way back.

Finally we found the cave. Yesterday, from the clearing to the cave took a half hour with Mr. Archer leading us. Today, from the clearing to the cave took nearly two hours by ourselves.

We stood outside the cave entrance and called, "Mr. Archer, are you in there?" No answer. We tried it again. I knocked on the rock with a stick. Still no answer.

"Do you suppose he went somewhere else?" Penny asked.

"Maybe he had to run away," I said. "Maybe someone was after him."

"Let's go inside and look," Penny finally said. She pulled the bushes back from the entrance, and I stepped in and tried to focus my eyes.

"Mr. Archer?" I said quietly. I didn't see or hear anything—until the groan. The sudden groan made me jump. "Mr. Archer?"

Another groan.

It wasn't a scary groan, like at Halloween. It was more like the kind you might hear in a hospital when you walk down the hall—or the groan when someone's dreaming a bad dream.

I still couldn't see anything—it was almost pitch black. Shuffling my feet and holding my hands out in front of me, I worked my way across the cave toward his bed. Then I knelt down and felt around me.

"What are you doing?" Penny whispered.

"I'm trying to get some light," I whispered back.

"Is he in the bed?"

"I can't tell. I'm getting some leaves to get the fire going." I picked up a handful of dried leaves, the way he had done yesterday, then crawled back to the fire area. I didn't have a stick to use like he did, so I felt around in the firepit carefully with my fingers. There'd been hot coals yesterday. Would there still be some today? Maybe

67

the fire was completely out. Maybe there wasn't a hot coal to be found.

"Ow!"

"What is it?" Penny said out loud.

"I just found a hot coal." I blew on the coal, just as he had. Soon it glowed bright red.

"I see some light," Penny whispered. "I can see your face."

I held a leaf against the hot coal and blew softly and steadily. "Catch," I said. Then prayed, *Please, God, let it catch fire.*

The leaf caught, and I put a couple of the others with it. With that little torch, I managed to get one tin-can lamp lit, then burned my fingers and had to drop the leaves. I stepped on them to put them out, then went back to the bed to get some more. He was lying there in his bed. "I think he's sick," I said. "Just look at him."

Mr. Archer's face was as white as the bellies of the bass we were catching. He was sweating. Every now and then he'd groan in pain.

As we stood there watching, he began to talk. He was talking strangely, not making sense—probably because of the pain.

"Listen," Penny said, her finger to her lips. He talked slowly and mumbled, but we could understand most of what he said.

"I tell you I didn't do it —I didn't sell your secrets to anyone—You have the wrong man . . . I'm innocent . . . Innocent . . ." His voice trailed off.

"What can we do?" I asked.

"The communicator," Penny said.

"Of course," I said, pulling it out of its case. I turned it on, but nothing happened. "It doesn't work," I said.

"Maybe it won't work in this cave," Penny suggested.

"Maybe." I went outside. The bright sunshine blinded me for a moment. I tried the machine again, just as Marsha had shown us. Nothing. "It doesn't work!" I shouted to Penny.

She stepped outside and tried the communicator herself, flicking switches on and off. "I'm going to try this one," she said, turning the forbidden dial.

"No!" I hissed. "That's the one we weren't supposed to touch!"

"Maybe we bumped the dial when we were hiking. Maybe that's why it doesn't work. Besides, it's not working anyway—we've got nothing to lose." She turned the forbidden dial slowly back and forth. Nothing.

We sank to our knees, both of us. "Now what?" I said.

"Do you think we can carry him out of here?" Penny asked.

"Just the two of us? No way."

"If we had a stretcher we could," she said. "He doesn't weigh very much."

"Maybe a helicopter will come over and drop us a stretcher," I said.

"Very funny."

We just knelt there for a minute, and then I said, "Maybe we could rig up a stretcher of some sort. We'd need poles—and something to stretch between them."

"There are poles over the fire pit," Penny said.

We ran back inside, stopping a moment to let our eyes adjust. I tipped the poles over and dragged the tops of them toward the lamp so I could see to untie the thong that held the three poles together. But the leather was pulled too tight. "I can't get this untied. Can you find his knife?"

Penny searched the cave, then looked at Mr. Archer. "It's still on his belt," she said, slipping the knife out of its sheath. "Yikes!" she screamed, throwing the knife toward me.

"What is it?"

"He grabbed my wrist."

"Is he awake?"

There was a pause as she bent over to look. "No. I don't think so."

While Penny unwrapped herself from Mr. Archer's grasp, I cut the thong and unwrapped the three poles. I picked the strongest-looking two of them. "But what do we put between them?" I asked. "Even if there was enough thong around here, we couldn't just tie him to the poles."

We searched around until finally Penny said, "The sleeping bag!"

"Yeah!"

Together we rolled him off it. We zipped and buttoned it, then cut holes in the bottom so we could poke the poles through. "Perfect," Penny said. "Now how are we going to get him onto it?"

"We'll put it here beside him, then roll him over onto it."

He didn't roll that easily. He jerked around and tried to hold on when we moved him. But we got him on the stretcher at last. Then he lay still.

Getting him through the cave entrance and around the bush was the hardest part. When we finally made it, we were already puffing. We still had several miles of woods to walk, carrying a stretcher. "Is there anything we need to take along?" Penny panted.

"No—well, how about the communicator?"

"It doesn't work," Penny reminded me—as if I needed reminding.

"Maybe it'll work back at the clearing."

"Take it then," Penny said. "But let's hurry. Just look at him."

We stopped every couple of minutes to catch our breath. I prayed the whole time—partly that he would live, and partly that we would be able to follow our birch twigs back out of the woods.

"I can't go any farther," Penny said at last, setting down her end of the stretcher.

"You have to. We have to."

"Maybe one of us should go for help," she said.

"And get lost? He might die. We have to keep going. Please."

"Okay. I'll try it again."

About five minutes later, as we were going down a slope, Penny stepped into a patch of slippery pine needles and lost her footing. She dropped her end of the stretcher—the foot end, luckily—and tumbled down the slope. At the bottom, she slammed the toes of her left foot hard against the stump of a pine tree.

She jumped and danced around on her right foot, holding her toes and crying. "Ow. Oh. *Ow!*"

"Are you okay?" I asked.

"Do I sound okay?" she barked angrily.

"Sorry. I mean, can you walk?"

"I don't know." She tried to and cried out in pain.

"I don't think it's much farther," I said. I was pretty sure we had gone in the right direction. I was also pretty sure that God was guiding us along our way, because we had managed to find our birch-twig trail markings pretty easily. "Let me run ahead and look. You count to ten, and then whistle. Then count to ten and whistle again. Keep whistling until I find my way back."

I was tireder than I'd ever been in my life, but I ran on ahead. I was right. The clearing wasn't more than half a block ahead. I ran back and told Penny. She had only whistled about three times.

"We don't have to go any farther," I said. "The clearing is just over that next rise."

"I wish we could get him closer," she said, "but my foot hurts."

"Are you sure you can't walk?"

She stood up and then just sank down again and groaned. She tried again, and this time, by keeping her weight on her heel, was able to walk slowly.

We picked up the stretcher and slowly carried it just inside the clearing. "This is close enough," I said.

We both stood there puffing, looking toward the road. The stretcher was behind us. "How are we going to get help?" Penny asked sadly.

"Who needs help?" came a voice from behind us.

8 Call In the Coast Guard

The voice was Mr. Archer's. He was awake.

"Where am I?" he asked weakly.

"You're at the edge of the clearing," I said.

"How did I get here?"

"We carried you," Penny said. "We made a stretcher."

"I don't know what's wrong with me," he said. "I think it may be appendicitis."

"We can't get help because our communicator doesn't work," Penny said.

"Let me see it," he asked. I kneeled down and handed him the communicator. He was so weak he dropped it. "Hold it up so I can see it, will you?"

I held the communicator in front of his face. "Ah," he said. "A Norman A–25. I know that model. Turn on the power switch." I turned on the switch, then turned the machine around again so he could see it. "No power," he said. "What's probably wrong is that . . . *AGHHHHHH!*"

He screamed again and writhed in pain, then seemed to faint again.

"He knew about the communicator," Penny said. "He was about to tell us how to fix it."

"If he doesn't wake up again," I said, "we'll have to get help some other way. Maybe I should walk out to the road and try to flag someone down."

"I guess you'll have to do the walking," she said, hobbling toward a tree to lean against.

"I'll get a couple of buckets to sit on," I said, running off toward the road. I brought them back, upended them, and we just sat there for a minute. Penny took off her left shoe and held her foot tenderly. I began to pray again. *Dear God,* I said, *please keep Mr. Archer alive long enough for help to get here—and please let him wake up long enough to show us how to get our communicator running.*

Sometimes after you pray, something happens and you wonder if that could be God's way of answering your prayer. Just as I was praying for a ranger pickup truck to show up—or a Forest Service helicopter—or at least for Mr. Archer to wake up and get our communicator going—what I got instead was a moose.

Across the clearing, as I happened to be looking in that direction, a moose stepped silently halfway into the open and just stood there, staring at us. I looked at it for a few seconds before my mind told me what I was seeing. "They're dangerous in mating season," Uncle Andrew had said. Was this mating season?

"Look," I whispered to Penny, pointing cautiously. I didn't want to make any quick or threatening moves.

"Wow," was all she could whisper.

We both stared. It was tall and brown, its coat sleek and shiny in the bright sun. He (she?) had no antlers like some moose have. Was it a cow moose, or was this the season moose lose their antlers? Antlers or no antlers, that animal was big enough to kill us all.

Nothing moved. "What if he comes over here?" Penny whispered. "We can run, but Mr. Archer can't."

I hadn't thought of that. We sat there and stared at that moose for what seemed like an hour. Finally I gave up. I remembered what Uncle Andrew had said about black bears. Maybe I could scare this moose away. I stood up slowly, reached under me for the wire handle of the pail I was sitting on, stood up, swung it around twice like a discus thrower, and heaved it in the direction of the moose. It landed about halfway between us with a hollow *boom*.

The moose turned and walked away. He just walked away.

"Yes!" Penny said, punching her fist to the sky. "You spooked him!"

"Chad the hero," I grinned. "Or maybe the moose just got bored."

We laughed in relief; then Penny pulled a handkerchief out of her pack, wet it with water from her canteen, and began to bathe Mr. Archer's forehead and face. It seemed to soothe him. His face relaxed. In less than a minute, his eyes opened again.

"Sorry," he said.

"Tell us about the Norman A–25 communicator," I said.

"Bouncing around in your pack sometimes loosens up the battery contacts," he said. "Take the back off and pull out the batteries." Penny held the communicator while I spun off two thumbscrews that held the panel over the batteries.

"Two batteries, right?" he whispered weakly. "Six-volt spring tops. Now. Stretch the springs out a bit, wet them with your tongue, and then slip them back in."

"Ow!" I said, getting a tiny shock from putting my tongue on the battery.

"One terminal at a time." He tried to smile. "Good sign, though. Power there."

When the batteries were back in and the back screwed on, Penny turned the communicator over and turned on the power switch. Now a light came on beside the switch. "Now it's working," she said.

"But you turned the frequency knob back in the cave," I said to Penny. "Remember?"

"Oh, no," she groaned.

"Hurry," he said. "I don't have much time. I can feel it. Turn the volume full on, switch it to 'listen,' hold it up to your ear, and turn the frequency knob very slowly from one end to the other."

When he had finished saying that, he gasped, thrashed around a little, and began to mumble deliriously: "I'm not going to jail for something I didn't do! There must be somebody else in the company . . ."

I stepped away from him so I could listen to the communicator. I ran back and forth on the frequency dial several times, then finally heard a sound. I turned the knob very carefully back and forth across that sound. The sound finally shaped itself into a voice—a woman's voice—and loud. I pulled it away from my ear.

"I've got something!" I shouted to Penny.

She limped over and knelt beside me. "Who is it?" she asked.

"I don't know, but it's a voice." When I had tuned the voice as loud as I could get it, I flipped the switch to "send" and shouted into the speaker, "Help us! We need help. *Mayday. Mayday.*"

"'Mayday'?" Penny said. "What do you mean— 'Mayday'? It's June."

"I heard it in a movie once," I explained. "I think it means *help*."

I flipped the switch to "listen." Nothing.

With the switch back on "send," we both shouted. "*Help! Send help. We have a sick man here who needs help—and right now! Mayday!*"

We flipped the switch and listened. There was static, then the same woman's voice, faintly: "Hear you, Mayday. Who are you? And where?"

Penny flipped the switch and said, "This is Penny and Chad. We have a very sick man here. Call the Marcell Ranger Station and have them send an ambulance to the clearing."

We flipped the switch and listened. "Heard you. Will call Marcell Ranger Station to send ambulance. Where is clearing?"

"They'll know," Penny said back. Then she asked, "Who is this?"

"Duluth Coast Guard," the woman said.

"Wow!" I whispered.

"I hope they can get through," Penny said.

"Me, too."

"Just for insurance," I said, "I think I should walk out to the highway."

"I'll keep bathing his forehead. That seems to soothe him. I'll keep trying the communicator, too."

It was a ten-minute walk out to the highway. When I got there, I leaned against a birch tree and waited. It was lonely. The waiting seemed like forever.

I didn't know which direction help would come from. I heard a car coming and ran up on the shoulder of the road. I waved frantically, but it wouldn't stop. She was a woman alone in a big, new car. Tourist, probably— just like me.

Finally I heard a faint sound from my left. The sound turned into the wail of a siren. Up the highway, flashing red lights appeared.

I waved the ambulance onto the logging road. They pulled in and stopped in a cloud of dust and exhaust. "Jump in," the woman in the passenger seat said, sliding over to make room.

"He's just ahead in the clearing," I said.

They drove into the clearing and spotted Penny and Mr. Archer right away. The driver made a wide U-turn, right over some of our seedlings. Funny how even with all of that going on, I still had time to hope the seedlings weren't crushed.

The paramedics both jumped out and suddenly were very busy. They checked Mr. Archer's pulse and breathing, mumbling things to each other. The woman ran to the ambulance and got their own stretcher, leaving our patchy sleeping bag and poles behind.

As they wheeled him over the rough ground to the back of the ambulance, she said, "You'd better jump in with us. We can't leave you out here alone."

We grabbed our packs and the communicator and hopped into the back of the ambulance with the woman. "You two sit up there in the corner, okay? I'm going to have to watch him every second."

"Where are we going?" Penny asked.

"Bigfork Hospital, for starters," she said. "He might have to go to Grand Rapids, or Duluth, or the Twin Cities," she said.

She pulled his jacket open, unbuttoned his jeans, and pushed her fingers into his belly. Mr. Archer winced. She reached into an ice chest for a cold pack. When she laid it on his belly, he winced again.

"Acute appendicitis," she muttered. "Maybe ruptured."

"That's what he thought," I said.

"He's quite some nature boy, isn't he?" she said with a smile. "We get a few of those around here."

She put her stethoscope to his neck and to his chest, then folded it back into her pocket. "Who is he, anyway?"

"We don't know. He didn't tell us."

"What's your uncle going to say," Penny whispered, "when he comes to the clearing and we aren't there?"

"Oh, wow. I don't know," I whispered back. We were talking softly, as if we were in a hospital. The back of this ambulance looked like a tiny hospital room.

"You need to contact someone?" the woman asked, overhearing us.

"My uncle. He'll worry."

"What's his name?" she asked.

"Andrew Buckworth," I answered. "He has a cabin on Horseshoe Lake."

"Andy? Sure, I know him," she said.

Did everyone know my uncle? "Maybe you should tell the Marcell Ranger Station, too," I added.

"Done," she said, knocking on the window and telling the driver. We heard him sending the message on the radio.

In ten minutes we were sitting in a hospital waiting room in Bigfork, eating cookies and drinking pop—and wondering what would happen next. We heard two nurses talking about him. "They think he's the guy who shot the kidnapper with an arrow," one said.

"Wow," the other nurse said, her eyebrows raised. I smiled. She said "wow" just like Penny does.

Bear Tracks Again

"Well, are you the two who brought in the Phantom of the Forest?" the doctor asked, pulling the green mask off his face and uncovering a pleasant smile.

"Yes sir," Penny answered.

"For starters, you saved his life. His appendix had ruptured. He was a real mess inside. Where did you find him?"

"He lives in a cave," I said.

"Did you just stumble onto the cave, or what?"

"He showed it to us," Penny said.

"Well, this is some story. This whole hospital's buzzing. Every nurse and orderly in this building has found some excuse to get into his room and have a look. Even a couple of the cooks have come up. Sounds like we may have visitors from the Twin Cities newspapers and TV stations. This is a great story." He flashed that smile at us again. "Oh, yes," he said after a pause. "I almost forgot. He was wearing these wooden clogs. Do you mind holding onto them for him? I'm afraid if I leave them unguarded, the souvenir hunters will get them."

He held them out, one for each of us. "Have you seen how he carved them?" he asked.

"He showed us," Penny said. "He made tracks for us in the woods."

"He's a special case, all right," the doctor said.

"Is he going to be okay?" Penny asked.

"I think so. Routine ruptured appendix. Fifty years ago, no hospital could have saved him. Fortunately, things are different now."

Just then my mother exploded into the little waiting room. "Oh, thank God!" she gasped. "You're all right, both of you!" She knelt and drew us both into a big hug. I hadn't seen Mom so excited since she sold lawyer Lundblad's house.

"Why did you think we *weren't* all right?" Penny asked.

"No one was around Andy's place when I arrived. I went in and there were no notes—nothing. I called the ranger station, and they said the last they heard the two of you were in an ambulance and on your way here to the Bigfork County Hospital."

"We were just riding with Mr. Archer," Penny explained. "His appendix raptured."

"*Rup*-tured," I said.

"Just keeping you on your toes," she smiled— then winced, and I remembered that her own toes were pretty sore.

"I was worried sick about the two of you," my mother went on. "I could have killed myself zooming up here on that winding road."

84

"We're glad you didn't," Penny said, patting Mom on the back in a motherly way. "So calm down. We're fine."

"Who's this Mr. Archer?" Mom asked the doctor.

Interrupting each other and sometimes all talking at once, the three of us told Mom that Mr. Archer was the one who had shot the kidnapper and saved Penny's Aunt Jean. We told her about his cave in the woods and everything else we knew about him—which, of course, didn't include his name, or where he came from, or why he was living out in the woods in the first place.

"Well, if the newspapers and TV report this, as I imagine they will," Mom said, "maybe someone will recognize his picture."

"With that beard?" the doctor said.

"This is certainly more exciting than sitting around at Andy's cabin," Mom said to Penny and me. She turned to the doctor again and asked, "When can we talk to him?"

"He'll be pretty groggy for several hours yet. Why don't you just come back about supper time? He'll be out of Intensive Care by then and in Room 105. Since he hasn't anyone else, I'll leave orders for only the three of you to visit. You'll be his family, okay?"

"Thanks," Penny said, standing up. "Ow!" she said as she put weight on her foot.

"What's the matter?" the doctor asked.

"I fell and banged my foot against a tree."

"Let's have a quick look," the doctor said. "Slip out of your shoe."

The doctor peeled off her sock and flexed her big toe around. "Ow," Penny said softly a couple of times.

"Let's run you into X-ray and take a quick picture. No charge," he smiled.

Five minutes later, Penny came back. With some difficulty and with a few groans, she managed to slip back into her sock and shoe.

"By the way," the doctor said to Mom as we were leaving, "you don't have to sit around at Andy's. Ask him to take you fishing. He's one of the best fishermen in this county."

"Is that doctor's orders?" Mom asked with a mock scowl. We all laughed.

"What *are* we going to do until supper time?" Mom asked as we stepped out into the bright afternoon sun.

"Fishing?" I said with a chuckle.

"Wish we had some way of finding out who your Mr. Archer really is," Mom said, looking thoughtful.

"Well, we could go back to his cave and look around," Penny suggested. "It wouldn't take us long to get there this time. Maybe we'll find some clues."

"How far is it?" Mom asked.

"About a fifteen-minute drive," I said, "and then a half-hour's walk."

"Assuming we don't get lost," Penny added.

"Can you walk that far?" Mom asked Penny.

"I can make it," Penny said.

In twenty minutes we were standing in the clearing. I watched Penny limp along the tracks the ambulance had made through our field of seedlings. She bent over and straightened up as many of the tiny trees as she could. "Most of them will be okay," she said.

Before we left for the cave, I rummaged around in Mom's glove compartment and found her flashlight and a book of matches. Before we left the clearing we showed Mom the stretcher we had used to carry Mr. Archer out of the woods.

"Clever, clever," she said.

I thought we should put his things back in the cave, so I pulled the poles out of the sleeping bag, wrapped the bag around the poles for a cushion, and put them over my shoulder.

We found our way to the cave easily this time. We pointed out to Mom the bushes that hid the entrance, and were about to step in when Penny pointed to the ground and said, "Look."

"Bear tracks," I whispered.

"But are those *really* bear tracks, or did your Mr. Archer make those with his wooden shoes?" Mom asked, also in a whisper.

"I don't know," I said, "but I don't remember seeing them here earlier."

"Do you suppose there's a real bear inside?" Penny asked.

"Why don't you just go in and see?" I said to Penny, risking a smile.

"Why don't *you*?" she returned without a pause.

"Not me," I said.

"Me neither," Penny said.

We stood there a minute or so, just staring at the cave entrance. "Well," Mom said, "I for one didn't come all this way just to turn around and go back. I want to see that cave. Besides, I don't think there's a real bear in there. I think those tracks were made by Mr. Archer. But just to be on the safe side," she said, "let me have the flashlight."

"Wait," I said, pulling the flashlight out of my back pocket. "Why don't we tie the flashlight on one of these poles and just sort of poke it into the cave?"

"Then you won't have to go in yourself," Penny agreed.

Mom knelt and pulled the lace out of one of her tennis shoes. She tied the flashlight to the smaller end of one of the poles, snapped it on, walked boldly to the bushes, then pushed the pole through the bushes and into the cave.

In no time at all, before any of us was ready, a bear exploded through the bush next to Mom with a huge roar.

I don't think the bear even touched Mom. I don't think it had a chance, because just as it crashed through the bushes and Penny and I instinctively yelled and lurched backward, Mom did a backflip. I mean a complete one, all the way over. She ended up on her stomach, looking at the cave entrance. The shoe without a lace was missing.

The bear just ran off into the woods. I've never seen Mom look so scared and surprised.

"Wow!" Penny said, running over to Mom. "Are you all right?"

"I think so," Mom said, rubbing her neck. "I haven't done a flip like that since junior-high gymnastics." She stood up and brushed off the pine needles and

leaves. "Ow!" she said, lifting up her shoeless foot and pulling a few pine needles out of her sock.

Her shoe was hanging in a tree over her head. I retrieved the pole, untied the flashlight, handed Mom the lace, and poked her shoe out of the tree.

By that time I had stopped shaking and started laughing. "What a flip you did!" I howled.

"Not funny," she said as she relaced her shoe and then stood up. "Now, let's go in," she said.

"Maybe there's another bear," I said.

"Just pull the bush back," Mom ordered. She sounded determined.

Penny and I pulled the bushes back while Mom shined the light into the cave.

"All clear," she said with a sigh of relief.

When we got inside, I used the matches to light the two tin-can lamps.

"Let's look for clues," Penny said.

The bear had made a mess, rummaging around in the berries and jerky. We looked over, around, and under everything. Finally Penny called out, "Look at this." Hidden inside a hollow birch log was a coffee can with a plastic lid.

"Careful," I said as she opened it.

"You think it's a bomb?" she scoffed. "It's just a little coffee can."

Mom shined the flashlight as Penny opened the can. Inside were a driver's license, a passport, and several newspaper clippings that had been folded and unfolded so often that they were splitting at the folds.

"Eureka!" I said. "Let's get these out into the sunlight and have a look."

When we dumped out the can, we also found a subpoena. "That's an order to appear in court," Mom explained. "That's probably when he ran away and went into hiding."

Wrapped inside one of the newspaper clippings I found a photo of a woman, pretty and young. She had signed it, "Love, Dee." I studied the picture. The woman looked like Penny. A *lot* like Penny.

It was time for us to leave if we were going to stop by the cabin and still get back to the hospital by suppertime. So we put everything back into the can and walked back to the car.

"Read the clippings to me as I drive," Mom said.

And that's how we found out that Mr. Archer's real name was Dr. John Walters. He was an electronics expert who had been accused by the corporation he worked for of selling some fiber-optics secrets to a rival company. The stories were dated in January, two-and-a-half years earlier.

The last clipping was brief. It just said that John Walters had disappeared.

Penny was going to read the subpoena, but she looked at it for a minute and then said, "*No* one could read that."

When we got back to the cabin, Uncle Andrew was there. "I've been searching *all over* for you," he said. "I went to the clearing, but the kids weren't there—just some makeshift stretcher. I got worried and called the Forest Service office. They told me you were at the Bigfork Hospital, so I followed all of you there. No one there, either. You had all disappeared."

"We went back to the clearing and hiked to his cave," Mom explained.

"Look at this," I said, pouring the contents of the can onto his kitchen table. He sat for a few minutes studying the driver's license and passport and reading the clippings and the subpoena. "Well, well. He was in some trouble," he muttered as he read. "But I wonder if any charges were ever brought. He was accused and subpoenaed, but nothing here says he was ever charged with any crime."

"Couldn't we call someone and ask?" Penny suggested.

"Who would we call?" I asked.

"You could start with the Twin Cities newspapers," Uncle Andrew said, opening a drawer and pulling out a thick telephone book. He dialed a number and handed the phone to Penny.

"Me?" she asked.

"Your idea," he whispered.

Penny told an operator she wanted to ask about the John Walters case from two years ago. "They're switching me over to their archivist," she said to us. "What's an archivist?"

"Kind of like the newspaper's librarian," Mom said.

But the archivist wasn't able to tell us anything we didn't already know from the clippings, so Mom called a friend at the Hennepin County Courthouse. "Pull the file on the John Walters case, can you?" There was a pause.

"Two years ago January," Mom said. Another pause. "Sure. Call us here." She gave the number.

We sat there over an hour, calling other numbers and waiting for calls. At last the phone rang and Penny grabbed it. After she hung up, she said, "Aha!"

"What?" I asked. "Who were you talking to?"

"Someone from the corporation he worked for. The public relations office. Someone else did it! Someone *had* sold secrets from their research, but it wasn't Mr. Archer—I mean, it wasn't John Walters! In fact, they're anxious to find him so they can apologize for accusing him in the first place. They also say they'll give him back pay for two years, and his job back if he wants it."

"What great news!" Mom said.

"Let's go tell him," I said.

"I think you should," Uncle Andrew said. "The three of you go ahead. I'll stay here and wait for the rest of the phone calls. We should have the whole story in another hour or so. Call me from the hospital."

The three of us drove north to Bigfork, all smiles and anticipation.

When we got to the hospital, we were practically running. We were so eager to tell John Walters-Archer that he was free. But when we got to Room 105 and opened the door, the room was empty. It didn't look like anyone had even used it.

"Where's the man who was supposed to be in Room 105?" Mother asked the station nurse.

"He's still in Intensive Care. We had a setback."

One Last Medical Problem

10

"So what's wrong?" Mom asked softly.

"His diet, I think," the doctor said. "Living out in the woods, eating only what he could hunt and gather, he was really low on several important minerals—including salt. The operation went fine, but he's gone into shock." He shook his head again and left the room.

"You're doing your best," Penny said, mostly to the empty doorway.

"We ought to call his family," Mom said, "now that we know who they are. They need to know he's—well, I was going to say they need to know he's all right. But he's not all right."

"I *hope* he'll be all right," Penny said sadly.

"Me, too," I said.

"I'll try to locate his family," Mom offered. "You two are his friends. Maybe you should just stay here and pray."

Mom came back about twenty minutes later. "It took some doing," she sighed, "but finally the company he worked for helped me find them. He has a mom and dad, a younger brother, and a fiancée."

"Fiancée?" Penny perked up.

"Her name is Dee, I'll bet," I said. "The one on the picture. The one who looks like Penny."

"That's right," Mom said. "They were planning to get married the summer after that horrible January. His mother said none of them ever gave up hope. They kept hoping that he would contact them so that they could tell him that his name had been cleared. But he never did."

"Are they coming here?" I asked.

"They're on their way. I had them talk with the doctor."

"Did the doctor say anything more?" Penny asked.

"He's called several specialists in the city," Mom said. "They're doing all they can."

"Thank goodness for the rescue squad," Penny sighed, "and for this little hospital—and for such a good doctor."

"And for you two," Mom added, "and that you were all so close by."

Mom called Uncle Andrew and told him we were spending the night at the hospital. We curled up in the waiting-room chairs and tried to nap. We did sleep a bit, but that ended at midnight when newspaper reporters started to show up.

They started to question us and write down notes. Then another group showed up—TV people with portable cameras. They interviewed all three of us. It was exciting, but we were tired and hungry, and I was starting to get mad that they were all so excited about their story and none of them seemed to care whether he lived or died.

The doctor looked in for a minute, then went out. He came back ten minutes later, when we were about to go crazy with all the questions and lights and cameras. "Come with me," the doctor said to the three of us.

"What's up?" the reporters shouted. "Is he awake? Can we see him?"

"You people might as well go get some sleep," the doctor said to them as gruffly as he could manage. "He's in critical condition. Even if he should get better during the night, and we should reclassify him as serious, or even stable, he won't have any visitors until late tomorrow afternoon at the earliest."

"Is that a promise?" one of the reporters asked.

"Come back tomorrow about two o'clock—after my rounds," the doctor said, then ushered the three of us down the hall. Then he turned us over to a nurse who led the way to a hospital room. We thought we were being taken to see Mr. Archer, but the room was empty.

"The doctor wanted you to have a private place, with no reporters, where you could get some rest. Use the beds. Relax. If you want anything to eat or drink, press this button."

"Thanks," Mom said.

Penny and I took pillows and curled up in a couple of the chairs. Mom flopped down on one of the beds. I didn't remember anything until about 7:00 A.M. when the same nurse came in with a tray of coffee, cocoa, juice, and breakfast rolls.

"Here's a little something to get you started," she said. "I'm going off duty now, but everyone on this floor knows who you are. When you're washed up and have

97

eaten, I think it would be good if you went into his room and sat with him. Sometimes unconscious patients respond to friendly voices and encouragement."

We washed and ate as quickly as we could; then we rang the nurses' station. They showed us into his room. As we walked, I noticed that Penny's limp wasn't any better.

We crowded around his bed, pulling up chairs. Penny held his hand and begged him to get better. "Please, please," she pleaded.

"I hope you can hear this and understand," Mom said in a soft voice, speaking to his quiet face and closed eyes. "I'm Chad's mom. Everyone here wants you to pull through. I called your family. Now listen to this: The charges against you have been dropped. Someone else stole the secrets. Your mom and dad are on their way here—and so is Dee." She said "Dee'" with extra emphasis.

There was no sign that he heard us. For the first time, it really sank in that he might not make it.

A nurse came in and we moved away so she could check. She put her fingers on his wrist and looked at her wristwatch. She put her stethoscope to his chest. She timed the drips in the two bags of liquid that were running into his wrists.

When she stepped back, Mom asked, "How is he?"

"About the same," she said. "I suppose that's good news. At least he isn't worse. Talk to him. Sing. Pray. Let him know someone cares."

We did all of those things. After that, it seemed like at least one of us was talking to him all the time.

We said everything we could think of. We prayed and we sang—but he just lay there silently.

Then I got an idea.

"We went back to your cave," I whispered near his ear. "We found your coffee can with the driver's license and passport and everything. You know what else we found?" I asked. "A bear. There was a bear in your cave. A real bear. It came bursting out and knocked Mom over in a somersault."

Slowly, a smile formed on his face. His eyes opened and he said, "No kidding? Really?"

His eyes closed again. Mom took one of his hands and rubbed it hard. "Stay with us," she said. "Stay awake."

"Please," Penny added.

"Call the nurse," Mom said to me.

When the nurse came in, we told her he had been awake for a moment.

"Good," she said, "because he has other visitors. Step out in the hall and meet them."

In the hall we met Mr. and Mrs. Walters and Dee. In person, Dee looked even *more* like Penny. Same color hair and eyes. There were hugs all around. Dee even kissed me on the forehead.

"Go in," Mom said. "We'll go back to the room we were using and wait there." Mom stepped over to the nurses' station and told them where we would be. "Let us know if there's any change, okay?"

About nine o'clock a nurse came in and said, "He's awake."

"Wonderful," Mom said. "Is he okay?"

"He's talking and listening," the nurse said. "Everyone's smiling. And he says he's hungry—that's the best sign."

We went to his room. The nurse said, "Go in—but just for a minute."

We went in. He turned and looked at us when we walked in. There were six of us now, all crowded around his bed.

"My family," he said. There were tears in his eyes as he glanced over the half circle of us. "All of you. My family."

"You'll all be in our wedding," Dee said.

"When will you be married?" Mom asked.

"How about tomorrow?" John said. We all laughed.

"That would be okay with me," Dee said when it was quiet enough to hear.

The nurse came in then and said we'd all have to leave for a while—they needed to examine John more thoroughly before he went back to sleep. "The doctor was here several times during the night. He says, pardon the joke, 'He's out of the woods.'" We all laughed again. "He says he'll look for you at 2:00 this afternoon when he comes back. He wants to meet the family."

"Why don't we all go to Andy's cabin 'til then?" Mom suggested. "We can relax there until it's time to come back."

"Maybe we can get away from the reporters there," Mr. Walters said. "They just about attacked us when we came in."

Mom telephoned and arranged everything. When we got there, Uncle Andrew had coffee and snacks ready for us. "We can have lunch in an hour," he said. "And if anyone wants to take a cool swim or a nap or anything, I have whatever you need."

A few minutes later, he said, "News time," snapping on the TV. "Let's see if all those reporters came up with anything."

John Walters was the lead story. They liked the doctor's name for him, apparently—they called him "The Phantom of the Forest." They showed old films and pictures from back when the secrets had been stolen. They interviewed people from his corporation, the boy who'd been saved from the mad dog—and even Penny's Aunt Jean.

"Wow!" Penny shouted, pointing to the screen. "That's my aunt!"

They had shots of us from the Bigfork Hospital. Penny and I and Mom were on, and so were Mr. and Mrs. Walters and Dee. "Look," Penny said. "There we are. On TV."

"John Walters is recovering," the newswoman said. "The doctor has promised our crew on-the-scene interviews this afternoon. There are rumors of book and movie representatives moving in to buy rights to his story. Watch Channel 11 Evening News as more of this exciting drama unfolds."

"You're all famous," Uncle Andrew said. We laughed.

When we got back to the hospital, reporters swarmed everywhere. "The doctor asked you to wait for him before you make any statements," the station nurse said to us.

"He's getting stronger by the minute," the doctor said when he came. "I've asked him, and he's willing to be rolled out into the hallway for a three-minute interview. Is that all right with the family?"

Mr. Walters said, "If John and you both think it will be all right, then we have no objections."

The reporters, of course, were still clamoring for more pictures and more questions when the three minutes were up, but the doctor was strict—he motioned the orderlies to push Mr. Walters' bed back into his room. We all went in right behind him, but only for a few minutes. Then we were asked to let him sleep and return in the evening.

Oddly, the TV and newspaper people had already disappeared when we came out. They were off filing their stories, I guess.

"I'd like to see his cave," Dee said to Penny and me when we got outside.

"Not me," Mom said. "I couldn't *bear* it."

Penny and I laughed until we could hardly stand up, and then we had to try to explain to Mr. and Mrs. Walters and Dee what had happened. "Really?" Mrs. Walters said, patting Mom on the shoulder. "A bear knocked you over?"

"Would you take me?" Dee asked. "Do we have time?"

"Sure," Penny said. "Anyone else want to go?"

"I guess not," Mrs. Walters said. "When I think of him living alone for two years—and all the time innocent—I just want to cry."

Mr. Walters put his arm around his wife's shoulders and whispered, "It's over now."

We all went back to the cabin. When Uncle Andrew heard that Dee and Penny and I were going back to the cave, he showed me how to light his gas lantern. "Take this," he said. "And I've got some flashlights, too."

As we were walking to the car, Dee noticed Penny limping. "What's wrong?" she asked.

"Nothing," Penny said.

"She banged her foot," I said.

"I'm okay," Penny grumbled. "Let's just go."

On our way to the cave, Penny said, "I have that same feeling I had when we were planting trees."

"What's that?" Dee asked.

"That someone is watching us."

We walked to the cave. No bear this time. I lit the lantern. It was so much brighter than Mr. Walters' little tin-can lanterns had been that we saw things we hadn't seen before—such as a carving, the face of a woman, faintly but very carefully scratched into one wall of the cave. Dee was fascinated. She studied every detail. After a minute Penny said to Dee, "It's you. It's the picture that was in the coffee can."

We had to tell her all about the coffee can we found, and what was in it.

Dee looked slowly all around her. "I wish I'd brought a camera," she said. "Two years." She shook her head. "What a waste."

I could see Penny thinking about that. After a moment she said to Dee, "It was maybe a waste for you, but not for everyone. He was here in the woods when a little boy needed him—and when my aunt needed him."

"I guess you're right," Dee said softly, and then began to cry. Penny went to her and hugged her.

"Thanks," Dee said. "I think we should leave now. I've seen enough."

That night we were all in John's hospital room when the early news came on. We all quieted down and watched. They told the whole story over again. We were all on TV again. The announcer told of offers from book publishers and movie producers. "Really?" Dee whispered to John. He just smiled and nodded.

The surprise was the cave. They had a film of John's cave. "They followed us," I said.

"That's what you were feeling," Dee said to Penny. "Someone *was* watching us."

When the news was over, the doctor came in carrying a clipboard. He greeted everyone and told us that John was doing fine but would need to stay in the hospital for several more days. And he said that we should leave now and let him rest.

As we were saying our good-byes, the doctor said, "Oh, by the way. There is one other medical condition I should tell you about." The room got very quiet. We thought John was still in some kind of danger.

The doctor pulled an X-ray film from his clipboard and held it up to the ceiling light. "Look at this," he said.

"That's not a stomach," John Walters said.

"That's a foot," Dee said.

"Guess whose?" the doctor said. There was silence. In all the excitement, we had all forgotten.

All except Penny. "Mine," she said softly.

"And here's the problem," the doctor pointed with his fingernail. "You have a broken toe."

"What do I do about that?" Penny asked.

"Nothing," the doctor smiled. "Toes have a way of healing all by themselves."

"Better than an appendix," John Walters—Mr. Archer—said to the doctor.

"Right you are," the doctor said, punching the Phantom of the Forest lightly on the shoulder. "Right you are."